Real Estate Investing:

The Advanced Guide to Real Estate Investing

(Learn the Secret Hints and Tips to Make Money in Today's Market)

© Copyright 2018 by - All rights reserved.

The following eBook is reproduced below with the goal of providing information that is as accurate and reliable as possible. Regardless, purchasing this eBook can be seen as consent to the fact that both the publisher and the author of this book are in no way experts on the topics discussed within and that any recommendations or suggestions that are made herein are for entertainment purposes only. Professionals should be consulted as needed prior to undertaking any of the action endorsed herein.

This declaration is deemed fair and valid by both the American Bar Association and the Committee of Publishers Association and is legally binding throughout the United States.

Furthermore, the transmission, duplication or reproduction of any of the following work including specific information will be considered an illegal act irrespective of whether it is done electronically or in print. This extends to creating a secondary or tertiary copy of the work or a recorded copy and is only allowed with express written consent from the Publisher. All additional rights reserved.

The information in the following pages is broadly considered to be a truthful and accurate account of facts and, as such, any inattention, use or misuse of the information in question by the reader will render any resulting actions solely under their purview. There are no scenarios in which the publisher or the original author of this work can be in any fashion deemed liable for any hardship or damages that may befall them after undertaking information described herein.

Additionally, the information in the following pages is intended only for informational purposes and should thus be thought of as universal. As befitting its nature, it is presented without assurance regarding its prolonged validity or interim quality. Trademarks that are mentioned are done without written consent and can in no way be considered an endorsement from the trademark holder.

Table of Contents

Introduction 5

Chapter 1: Real Estate vs. the Stock Market 8

Chapter 2: Attracting Lenders 27

Chapter 3: Protecting Your Assets 42

Chapter 4: Direct Ownership Real Estate

    Investment 54

Chapter 5: Real Estate Investment Groups

    and Limited Partnerships 81

Chapter 6: Real Estate Investment Trusts 85

Conclusion 90

Introduction

Congratulations on downloading this book and thank you for doing so.

The following chapters will discuss how you can invest your money and put it to work for you to create a better future for you and your family.

Are you like most of us, tired of your day job and wishing that something better would come along? Are you struggling every month to make ends meet and wondering what you can do to help yourself? Are you just in need of some passive income for retirement? Do you have extra money in the bank that you wish would earn higher returns than the bank pays?

If you answered yes to any of these questions, then this book is for you. This book will tell you how you can get involved in real estate at any level of investment and spend only as much time as you want to spend on it.

You will learn all the secrets the banks don't want you to know about how you can get approved for the loans you need so that you can get started investing in real estate with little to no upfront money.

You will learn how to make sure that your personal assets are protected in an uncertain world so that you can enjoy peace of mind, even if the worst happens.

You will learn all you need to know about the different kinds of real estate investments that are out there, as well as the risks and rewards for each, so that you can make the best decision for you and your family. You will also learn what level of personal involvement is required by each so that you can find the perfect match for your level of interest in real estate.

Whether your interest in real estate investment is purely casual or you are thinking of making it a second career, this book will be your ultimate guide to get started.

There are plenty of books on this subject on the market, thanks again for choosing this one! Every effort was made to ensure it is full of as much useful information as possible. Please enjoy!

Chapter 1:
Real Estate vs. the Stock Market

Prior to the start of the Industrial Revolution, wealth was mostly measured in precious metals like gold and silver, livestock like cattle and sheep, and land. If you wanted to invest your money, those were your main options. During the Industrial Revolution, large companies came to be publicly owned and traded. Shares of ownership of these companies are called stock and are bought and sold on stock markets. This introduced a new way for those with extra money to invest it and make it grow.

So, you have some extra money, and you are looking for the best way to invest it. People frequently wonder which is better in today's world—real estate or the stock market. Unfortunately, there is no easy answer to this. Is a Mercedes Benz better than a BMW? Is prime rib better than veal? It's simply a matter of preference. It also comes down to the specifics of each individual investment. There are no universal rules in investing your money; you must carefully examine each opportunity and decide for yourself whether it is right for you. After all, this is *your* hard-earned money, and nobody will protect it better than you.

Neither real estate nor the stock market is better than the other. They are simply different. But that is not to say that the choice between the two doesn't matter; each investor must decide for himself which option best matches their short-term and long-term investment strategy.

If you had been in a position to buy up a bunch of beachfront property in the 1960s and 1970s prior to the California real estate explosion, very few stocks could compete with the returns over a couple decades.

And what real estate on Earth could compete with the returns if you had invested in shares of Microsoft, Facebook or Walmart in the early days, especially if you just kept rolling over your dividends? So, the answer is not a one-size-fits-all. The most successful investors have a diverse portfolio that includes stock and real estate investments.

Let's dive in by taking a look at both kinds of investment:

Real Estate: When investing in real estate, all you are doing is buying a piece of physical land or property. Some real estate takes money out of your pocket every month that you own it—for example, a vacant lot that you will sell one day to a developer, but, in the meantime, you are still paying taxes, maintenance, etc. Some real estate brings money in—for example, an apartment building, rental houses or a commercial building where the occupants are sending you money each month. You use that money to pay any expenses, and the difference is your profit each month.

Stocks: When you buy shares of stock, you are buying part of a company. Whether that company makes TVs, cell phones or bread or sells cars or develops new apps, as one of the owners you get a share of any profit that company earns. The more stock you own the higher your share of the profit. The stock market may seem complicated, but it couldn't be easier. If a company has issued 10,000 stocks and you own 1,000 of them, you own 10% of that company. Therefore, every year the company pays out dividends, as a 10% owner of that company you will receive 10% of the payout. As a 10% owner, you will also have 10% of the say over how the company is to be run.

Real Estate vs. Stocks – Pros and Cons

Now we will discuss the pros and cons of each of these to give you a better understanding of which better matches your investing goals.

Real estate pros:

The average person usually finds real estate to be a more comfortable investment to get started. Children of the American working and middle classes often grow up hearing their parents emphasize the importance of home ownership, while upper-class children often hear discussions of the stock market during their formative years. The result is that the middle class is more likely to invest in real estate than they are in stocks or bonds.

When you invest in real estate, you're investing in something real and solid. You can drive up to it and see and touch it, you can take photos of it to show your friends, you have the feeling of pride of ownership. It's *yours.* Many investors find that important when looking into where to put their money because we work hard for our money and we want something to show for it. Because they only represent an *idea,* a share of ownership in a company, it may be hard for many to see any value in a stock certificate.

Borrowing money to invest in real estate can be much safer than borrowing money to buy stock (margin trading) due to the different ways the loans are structured.

Compared to stocks, it's much harder to be ripped off in real estate. If you do your homework and go examine the property itself, make your own repairs, vet your tenants yourself, you will not be taken by surprise. It's hard to hide deception in real estate; the property is either there and in the advertised condition or not. With stocks, you kind of just have to take everybody at their word and trust that the management of the company knows their business and that the auditors are on the ball. This can be unsettling for many investors.

Real estate investments are a great way to protect yourself against inflation in the long term.

Inflation happens when the government puts new dollars into circulation, thereby watering down the value of the other dollars already in circulation. When that happens, the cost of almost all goods, including real estate, increases to offset the inflation. Plus, if it is a rental property the cost of rent will increase over time. It is not that these properties necessarily increase in value; you as the owner are simply raising the prices to occupy and use the property to offset the lower value of the dollar.

If one of your primary goals in investing is to protect your savings against the government's rampant printing of new money to service international debts, real estate may be ideal for you. As Mark Twain once said, "Buy land, they're not making it anymore!"

Real estate cons:

In comparison with stocks, real estate requires a lot of time. When you buy a stock, your work is pretty much done. You can simply put it into a safe deposit box and wait until the dividends, if any, come to you. As a real estate owner, you are on call 24/7 if something goes wrong with one of your units like a clogged toilet, gas leak or a fire, and you are liable to get sued if somebody is injured on your property. Even if you hire a property manager or are only involved in real estate as an investor, you will still have to attend meetings and otherwise invest time that stocks do not require.

As mentioned above, if one of your properties is unoccupied it will cost you money to own it. You will still have to pay Uncle Sam his taxes every month, as well as any maintenance costs, utilities, insurance, and countless other things you likely haven't thought of yet. So, if circumstances beyond your control cause a higher than expected vacancy rate in your units, you could easily lose money! At the end of the day, an empty building is worth nothing to you.

For the most part, real estate does not really increase in value after adjusting for inflation. As we discussed above, real estate is great protection against inflation, but the real value of real estate rarely increases faster than inflation. How does this work? Let's say you invest $20,000 of your own money in buying a $100,000 house, borrowing the other $80,000. With an inflation rate of only 3%, the house you bought for $100,000 is now worth $103,000, not because the real "value" increased but because it now takes 3% more dollars to purchase anything due to inflation. But you only invested $20,000, so that means you earned $3,000 from a $20,000 investment or a 15% return! Taking inflation into account, that is a 12% return before taking ownership expenses into account. This attractive return on investment is what makes real estate so intriguing.

Stock market pros:

Nearly all research has proven that buying stocks, reinvesting your profits into more stocks, and holding your stocks long term is the greatest creator of wealth yet invented, even accounting for all the crashes. No other asset brings money in like owning a business, and when you own stocks, you own part of a business. But, while running your own small business requires a large investment of your time, owning part of a business in the form of stocks only requires a little homework upfront to make sure the company is a good fit for you. Professional managers watched over by a board of directors run the company. You get the benefits of their work without having to show up at the offices every day. This is truly passive income.

If you had invested only $1,000 in Amazon when it went public in 1997 (remember, at that time it was only an online bookstore), you would now have over $480,000 worth of stock, and that's if you didn't roll your earnings back into the company! That's right—a return on investment of over 48,000 percent over only a couple of decades. On top of that, you would also have your yearly cash dividend payout coming in every year with no effort on your part.

It is much easier to diversify when investing in stocks than when investing in real estate. Some mutual funds only require you to invest as little as a hundred bucks a month, and some companies let you invest in dozens of different companies for a flat rate as low as only a few dollars a month. Even the smallest real estate investment requires much more than $100. Real estate usually represents a pretty significant investment for most folks.

In case you need cash quick, it is far easier to cash out of stocks than it is with real estate. During normal trading hours, you can sell your entire stock portfolio in a matter of moments if you wish to. Trying to sell a piece of real estate is a process that can take days, months or even years in some cases.

It is also a lot easier to borrow against stocks than real estate. You can simply write a check against your stock trading account once a broker has approved you for margin borrowing. (Margin borrowing is simply borrowing money against stocks that you already own to purchase more stocks in the expectation that the new stocks will increase in value more than the interest you will pay the lender.)

Stock market cons:

In spite of their proven long-term ability to create more wealth, most stock market investors are unable to benefit from this. This is because people, by nature, are fickle, undisciplined and prone to panic when it comes to investing. These folks actually end up losing money in the market because of fear and a sort of herd instinct. For example, during the most recent financial collapse in the late 2000s, many investors panicked and sold their shares at a time when the market had lost over half of its value—the exact wrong strategy. Disciplined investors buy when the market is at its lowest and everyone else is panicking.

The stock market can be volatile. Stock prices will soar and crash in the short term. Your $100 investment may go to $500 one day then to $50 the next. If you did your homework before buying that stock, this shouldn't concern you; you may even see this as a chance to double down when the stock is at its lowest and buy more or cash out part of your investment when it reaches its high point, if you think the stock is overvalued at that price.

When looking at growth charts, stocks seem like they have not really done anything for the past decade. They may seem stagnant and like a low-yield investment. But this is because growth charts don't take reinvested dividends into account. As mentioned above, every year a profitable company sends its shareholders a check for their percentage of the profits; this is the dividend check. The canny investor reinvests these dividends into the company by using them to purchase more stock so that his dividend checks get larger every year.

You now have a pretty good overview of the differences between the stock market and real estate investment. As mentioned, both are great investments, and your long-term goal should be to have a diverse portfolio that consists of both stocks and real estate.

But this book concerns real estate investment, so if you've made it this far and real estate investing still seems like a good fit for you, read on to discover how to get started.

For most people, real estate is the easiest investment to understand because there is an exchange of money for a tangible good. This is appealing because it is simple and straightforward. As long as the rent comes in every month from the tenant and the landlord keeps the water flowing and toilet flushing, everybody wins. However, investing in real estate can be more complicated than this. This is because there are several kinds of real estate investment, ranging from industrial to residential, and even some real estate that trades on stock exchanges. This book was written to help you wade through the options.

To put it as simply as possible, the goal when investing in real estate is to put your money to work for you at once so that it will grow into more money down the road. Your profit, or "return on investment" (ROI), must be enough to cover all of your ownership costs while still providing enough to make your risk worthwhile.

Investing in real estate can be as simple as playing Monopoly when you have a grasp of the basic factors of economics, investment, and risk.

To win, you buy properties, avoid bankruptcy, and generate rent so that you can buy more properties and start the cycle again. However, remember that simple is not the same as easy or without risk. If you lose at this game, the long-term consequences can be disastrous. You could even end up bankrupt.

There are several ways for you to make money from real estate. This is why it's such a great investment in the right market.

Incoming rent. This is, perhaps, the most common type of real estate investment. You invest in a property, such as an apartment building, and every month your tenants send you money in exchange for being allowed to occupy one of your units. But this does not just have to be residential properties; this can include office buildings, laundromats, storage units, restaurants, really anything that someone may want to lease from you for a certain period of time. This is probably the most time-consuming kind of real estate investment, but it can be an ongoing source of income.

Appreciation. Appreciation is when the value of your property increases due to a boom in the real estate market, your neighborhood suddenly becoming gentrified, a large popular business moving into the neighborhood, increasing commercial traffic, or you investing time and effort to make improvements to the property, making it more appealing to potential renters or buyers. Relying on appreciation for you to make a return on your investment can be difficult. It is often impossible to know which will be the next desirable neighborhood or how buyers will react to any change in the neighborhood or in the property itself. It can be quite profitable, but it is certainly not as safe as rental income.

Act as a middleman. In almost any real estate transaction, money doesn't just pass between buyer and seller. There are people who specialize in the real estate industry and make your life easier during the transaction in exchange for a percentage of the sale price, this can include real estate agents, who advertise your home and negotiate the sale for you. There are real estate brokers, who make a commission from each property that is sold, or property management companies, who will manage your rental properties for you in exchange for a percentage of the income. For example, the property management company earns a certain percentage of the tenants' rent payments in exchange for taking care of all the maintenance, fixing what needs to be fixed, keeping the grounds looking nice, finding good tenants, etc. A very fair deal, actually.

Miscellaneous Real Estate Income. If you own an apartment complex, perhaps you have a laundry room where tenants can safely wash their clothes near to their home in exchange for a few quarters. Maybe you have vending machines in your office buildings to provide snacks to the employees there. Arcade video games in the lobbies of restaurants. These are the kinds of other sources of real estate income that are often overlooked.

Ways to get a return on investment from your properties are only limited by your imagination.

Hopefully, now you are excited about the potential that investing in real estate can hold. But to invest in real estate you need money, usually more money than you will have available. Fortunately, there are numerous lenders you can apply to for a loan. Our next chapter will focus on how to make yourself stand out when lenders are reviewing your loan application.

Chapter 2:
Attracting Lenders

There are several ways to make your first investment in real estate. If you want to purchase a property, you can use debt by taking a mortgage out of that property, as though you already own it. This is often called "leverage," and it attracts many real estate investors because it allows them to acquire properties that they could not afford to buy otherwise. However, there are no guarantees in life, so using debt to purchase real estate can turn to disaster in a failing real estate market because the investor will still be required to make all mortgage payments, and that road can lead to bankruptcy.

As previously discussed, one of the main benefits of real estate investing vs. the stock market is the ability to acquire an investment property with relatively little money down and borrow the rest. But just like any other loan, this does require you to find somebody (usually a bank) who will lend you the money you need to start your investment career. That is why this chapter will focus on maximizing your borrowing potential.

First and foremost, take a realistic look at your finances. How much extra income do you actually have? Investing in any market is a gamble. If it was foolproof, the world would be made of millionaires. Make sure that you can afford to lose any money that you invest, and, especially when investing in real estate, make sure you will be able to afford to pay all of the monthly costs that come with owning that property until you find a tenant; this could take months in some cases.

Claim every penny of income that you can throughout the year, even cash payments. Of course, it is tempting not to report certain income, even if not legal, and nobody enjoys paying taxes if they can avoid it. But when it comes to trying to borrow money from a bank, that will seriously limit your borrowing potential. All the bank cares about is whether you can pay back their money. More income means you are a better credit risk. Plain and simple.

Banks don't just go back a couple of months when evaluating a loan request; they go back a couple of years. The more money you are reporting as income the more favorably they will view your request. Of course, you must pay taxes on any declared income, but you will seem stabler and like a better risk.

Reduce your available credit. As strange as it sounds, having a high credit limit with credit cards can hurt your borrowing potential.

Let's say that you have $40,000 in available credit spread out over several credit cards. You don't actually use the cards; you just have them in case of emergency. These high limits will actually lower your borrowing potential with banks. Why? Because even if you have not spent one dollar with these credit cards, the bank sees them as $40,000 in debt, because at any time after the loan is issued you *could* use them, and now you have an additional $40,000 in debt versus likely a similar amount of income.

Even making minimum payments on the credit cards at around 3% that is an additional $1,200 of expense for you each month So, banks err on the side of caution and treat that *potential* debt as a real debt; in other words, they take that $1,200 dollars away from your money available to repay their loan. This, of course, results in a smaller loan. So, if you have credit cards that you don't need, either pay them down or get rid of them altogether. This simple step will make you look much more attractive to lenders.

Make sure your tax returns are correct. As already discussed, banks look at the last two tax returns to determine your income. If your taxes are correct, up to date and include all income, this will show you as a stable person with a steady income—exactly the kind of folks banks want to lend to.

Split your expenses with your partner. If you have a partner whose name is not going to be on the mortgage, it can often be helpful to split expenses with them. Instead of paying for all of the monthly bills, allow your partner to pay for half of them. This will indicate to banks that your monthly expenses have room for a higher loan-repayment amount. There are some legalities when it comes to doing this, so make sure you speak with a tax accountant or a similar professional before getting started.

Find a lender who specializes in your kind of income. There are numerous ways to make a legitimate living. Not everyone has a nine-to-five job Monday through Friday. There are contractors, small business owners, Uber drivers, and the list goes on and on. Different lenders favor different types of income.

When choosing a lender, make sure you find one that specializes in your type of income. Otherwise, you are reducing the amount of money you will be able to borrow.

Find a lender who takes rental income into consideration. Unfortunately, not all banks or lenders will take rental income from an investment property into account. Some count none of the rent, others will take a very small percentage into consideration, but some will take 80% or more into account. Obviously, the more of the rent they will take into account as a means of repayment the higher the loan amount you will qualify for. So, we are beginning to see that the choice of lender can be a crucial one, in more ways than one.

Shop around for your loan. Finding the right lender is critical as well because you want to find the lowest interest rate you can. Every 1% of interest equals $1,000 per year for every $100,000 of the loan. That is money you could be using to pay off the loan early or to invest in new properties. Therefore, it is well worth the investment of time to shop around until finding the best interest rate you can.

Find the right type of loan for you. As strange as it sounds, even within the same bank or lending institution the interest rates can vary based on the type of loan you take out. The best way to look into this is to speak to your banker or mortgage broker about what your borrowing potential will be with each type of loan.

Use other properties as collateral. If you own other properties, include them in the mortgage as collateral. This will give banks the peace of mind of knowing they can recoup their losses if everything goes belly up on the loan. Of course, this is also a risky strategy because, if the real estate market shifts against you, the bank could force you to sell the property to service the loan.

Another great strategy can be an interest-only loan. With interest loans, the borrower is allowed for a set period of time (5–10 years, usually, in the US) to pay only the interest on the mortgage. This means a lower monthly payment, so it will allow you to finance more debt under this strategy than if you had to repay the interest and principal in the beginning. This sort of loan is riskier for lenders, so they will usually charge a slightly higher interest rate.

This can also be accomplished by extending the length of the mortgage with a traditional principal and interest model. The monthly payment for a 30-year loan will be lower than a 20-year loan, which will again raise your borrowing potential.

Roll credit card debt into your mortgage. This is a risky strategy that can be more expensive in the long run, but another effective strategy can be to roll all of your credit card debt into a mortgage. If you are paying 20% on your credit card debt but only 5% on your mortgage, that extra 15% will show up to lenders as money that can be used to repay their loan, thus increasing your borrowing potential. This should not be done, however, if you are planning on keeping the property long term because over the life of the mortgage you will pay much more in interest than you would have had you simply paid off the credit card debt over 3–5 years. Additionally, if you default on credit card debt, the worst the lender can do is ding your credit report and pester you with phone calls; if you default on a mortgage, they can take your house away. However, if this is a short-term investment, such as a fix and flip, this can be a great strategy.

Save up your money for a larger down payment. While it may not be fast, this is a fantastic way to maximize your borrowing potential. If you can only put up less than 20% of the value of the property, you will be required to buy Private Mortgage Insurance (PMI). This is insurance to cover any losses to the lender if you are unable to service the debt and the lender cannot recoup all of their investment in a sale. The banks will take this cost into account when calculating how much debt you can afford to service, so if you can save up 21% of the cost as a deposit, that will do away with the need to pay for PMI every month and increase your borrowing power.

While you're saving up your money for the down payment on a property, how should you invest that money to earn a return on it? The answer is *don't*. Don't risk this money; this is your real estate future. Instead, put your money somewhere safe, like a federally insured bank. This is the time to practice something called capital preservation.

More people lose their money trying to squeeze a couple extra percentage points of profit out of it than by any other mistake. When it comes to money that you need for a specific purpose, such as your down payment, you must always keep your eye on the prize. Don't get distracted by shiny, new investments.

These savings need to be readily accessible to you within a few days at the most. This is money that is not supposed to be earning a return because it is designated for a specific purpose and you don't want to risk it. Your *extra* money is what is supposed to grow your wealth. This is called capital. It's the money you have set aside for investment purposes.

For example, the money you put into your 401(k) at work every month would be considered retirement capital as it is set aside to finance your retirement. The money you save at work through a 401(k) or 403(b) plan, for instance, would be considered retirement capital.

Most financial catastrophes have arisen from a well-meant decision to take on more financial risk than the investor could afford. It's easy to talk yourself into, and when you overextend yourself you are certain that it will all work out, but what if it doesn't? What if it goes wrong? The consequences will be financially devastating.

So, where should you keep your down payment? There are really only a few options to keep your money safe until the magical day when you have enough to begin your career as a real estate investor:

FDIC Insured Banks

You can put your money in a checking or savings account at any FDIC member bank. Your bank is almost certainly an FDIC member, and if you are not sure, look for the sticker on their window or just ask. The benefits of a bank are that you can access your money anytime during normal banking hours and there is no penalty for taking it out. Plus, if the bank fails, your money is completely insured by the government, up to $100,000.

FDIC Insured Certificates of Deposit (CDs)

CDs are offered by many FDIC members, such as local banks. A certificate of deposit is essentially a loan by you to the bank for a specific length of time in exchange for a guaranteed return on your investment. Normally, the rewards will be higher when the loan is for a longer period of time. If you are not going to be needing your money for a while, this can be a good option while offering higher returns than a simple bank account.

This is a poor choice if there is a possibility that you will need your money sooner than the duration of the loan to the bank. If you do withdraw your money early, there can be significant financial penalties, so make sure you will not need that money until the CD expires.

U.S. Treasury Bills (T-Bills)

T-Bills are debts from the US government that mature after one year or less. T-Bills are considered absolutely safe because they are fully backed by the United States government so a default is unthinkable. Treasury bills are sold at a lower rate than face value, but once they mature you receive the full face value. This only really makes sense for larger amounts of money over $10,000.

Money Market Accounts

A Money Market Account (MMA) is nothing more than a savings account at your local bank. (MMAs are *not* the same as a Money Market Fund, which is a sort of mutual fund investment.) MMAs typically earn a much higher interest rate than a traditional savings account because you are authorizing the bank to use that money for its own investments. The ability to transfer that money is a little more limited, but since you are not going to be using that money it should not matter. There is a minimum deposit required from $500 all the way up to $5,000. These accounts are usually FDIC insured, just like any other savings account, which protects you if your bank fails. Before investing in an MMA, **always** double check with your bank that it is FDIC insured; if not, keep looking.

U.S. Savings Bonds

There are two main types of United States savings bonds: Series I and Series EE. Each has its own benefits, but if you don't need your money for at least a year, they may be ideal for you because you are guaranteed never to lose money on your investment. This is the peace of mind you need when you are storing money that you need, like that down payment for your real estate dreams.

Chapter 3:
Protecting Your Assets

Real estate is a risky business and, above all, your personal assets must be protected. If somebody gets personally injured due to a defect in one of your buildings, you don't want them to be able to sue you personally. This first part is very important, and it will be repeated. You do not invest in real estate in your own name when purchasing properties. Not ever, if you can avoid it. Instead, to protect your personal wealth, look into forming a legal structure known as an LLC, or Limited Liability Company, or another form of limited partnership. Usually, when something goes wrong, only the assets of the LLC or of the partnership can be forfeited, not those of the members. So, if, for example, one of your investments goes belly up or someone slips and falls in your business, the worst case scenario is that you lose your investment, not everything you own. This is why I will stress *do not buy real estate investments in your own name!*

Recently, such Limited Liability Companies have become popular methods for small investors to own parts of family businesses or new companies. The protections and benefits they provide to the members of the LLC leave no doubt as to why they have exploded in popularity among investors. As a new investor, it is crucial for you to understand LLCs and how they will impact your taxes.

So, what exactly is an LLC? In a nutshell, a Limited Liability Company is a sort of cross between a partnership and a corporation. You get the simplicity and tax breaks of a partnership with all the personal asset protection of a corporation.

The owners of a Limited Liability Company are referred to officially as the "members". A Limited Liability Company can have one member or many, as many as you want. Under an LLC structure, the members' personal assets are protected from being seized by the company's debt holders.

LLCs are relatively new entities, only appearing for the first time around four decades ago. Today, they are the fastest growing type of new business entity. We will discuss the pros and cons of forming an LLC to help you decide whether it is right for you.

Limited Liability Company pros:

There are a number of advantages to structuring your company as an LLC. These include:

Limited Liability

Members cannot be held personally liable for any actions that the company takes. As previously discussed, this means that, as a member of an LLC, your personal assets (cars, bank accounts, 401(k), your home) are safe if the company owes money to a creditor. If you decide that a Limited Liability Company is the right option for you, make sure you keep your personal and business finances totally separate and run your company legitimately because you could lose this protection otherwise.

Pass-Through Federal Taxation

By default, a Limited Liability Company is considered by the IRS to be a pass-through entity. This means that any profits will go straight to the members without being taxed at the corporate level by the government. Instead, members declare these profits on their personal income tax returns. This makes filing taxes much simpler, and if there are no profits, members can list those losses to offset their tax burdens.

Simple to Get Started

Compared to forming a new corporation, forming a Limited Liability Company is quite easy and the fees are much lower, though this does vary state by state. You should absolutely consult with an attorney or an accountant to make sure that a Limited Liability Company is a good option for your individual circumstances, but once you decide to form one, you should be able to manage the paperwork without an outside specialist. This will save you more money to invest in a down payment.

You Can Manage It Yourself

One of the problems with a corporation is that it must be managed by an elected board of directors. This problem is completely solved by a Limited Liability Company. This is because a Limited Liability Company offers much greater flexibility when deciding what sort of management you would like to have running your company. You can decide that the LLC will be managed by its members (you, in other words) or you can choose to bring in professional managers from outside if you prefer to be more hands-off.

Some states even consider a Limited Liability Company member-managed by default, unless the LLC's filings with the state request otherwise. Remember, a Limited Liability Company can even consist of only one member, so if you prefer to give no other member control over how your money is invested, you can be the only member of the Limited Liability Company. This is not recommended, however, because it will limit the pool of money that is available to be invested in your extra income.

Limited Liability Company cons:

We can see that a Limited Liability Company has some significant advantages, but it may not be right for every investor. There are some drawbacks, so before you decide how you're going to organize your company, let's discuss some of them.

Membership Turnover Has Consequences

This is one of the more problematic drawbacks of a Limited Liability Company. There are many states in the US where if a member dies, goes bankrupt or otherwise leaves the company, the Limited Liability Company itself must be completely broken up, and the remaining members must fulfill any remaining financial or legal obligations necessary to dissolve the business. The remaining members can still do business, naturally, but they will have to form an entirely new Limited Liability Company to do so as before.

A Limited Liability Company Does Have Limits

Even if your company has been set up as a Limited Liability Company, the courts can still decide that your Limited Liability Company cannot protect your personal assets. If you are not careful to keep your business finances separate from your personal finances, or if the judge decides that you have run your company fraudulently and harmed others by doing so, the courts can "pierce the corporate veil," meaning your personal assets can be seized. So, if you do decide to organize your company under a Limited Liability Company, make sure you keep your financial transactions separate and always act in good faith with those you are doing business with. (Good advice in daily life too.)

Taxes

Unless the Limited Liability Company requests otherwise, the IRS will consider the company as a partnership for tax purposes unless the company chooses to be taxed as a corporation. What this means is that the members working for the Limited Liability Company are considered to be self-employed. Those self-employed members are fully responsible for paying Medicare and Social Security taxes personally. This is known as self-employment tax, and members are taxed based upon the Limited Liability Company's net profits if any. However, if your Limited Liability Company chooses to be taxed as an S Corporation, members who work for the company are only taxed based upon your actual compensation from the company, not the company's net earnings. Which of these options will work best for your particular circumstances must be discussed by you and a qualified accountant.

Getting Started

Once you have decided whether a Limited Liability Company is the right choice for you, it is quite easy to get started.

First, simply choose a name for your company. Register a name that has not already been used in the state where you plan to do business. You can use online searches, the county clerk and your state's secretary of state to make sure that your name has not already been taken. Make sure you do this in all states where you plan to do business.

Next, select a registered agent for your Limited Liability Company. This is the person the members select to represent the Limited Liability Company in all official correspondence. Most states require the name and address of the registered agent be listed on the filing application as all official correspondence will be addressed to that person. Your Limited Liability Company may choose to have a member serve in this capacity in most states or you may choose to hire a third-party company that specializes in registered-agent services.

Third, draw up your partnership agreement. If you are the only member of the Limited Liability Company, you may skip this step, but most readers will be interested in pooling their resources with other like-minded investors, and this step is crucial. It is not required by law, but you and the other members should certainly develop a written agreement that outlines exactly how the company will be managed, who owns what percentage of the company, voting structures, who will be responsible for what duties within the company, profit and loss distribution, etc. In other words, try to solve any potential problems in advance in writing with the other members so that everyone is on the same page from day one. This will help to avoid difficult conversations between the members down the road.

After that, file your articles of organization. This is what will make your Limited Liability Company official in the state's eyes. Most states require basic information such as the name, management type, principal place of business, etc. If you have planned your business thoroughly, these questions will present no problem.

Obtain your employer ID number. Since you will be operating as a partnership if you elect to set up a Limited Liability Company, the IRS will require you to have an EIN. This number will be required by the IRS for tax purposes, so don't forget this step!

Finally, we have already discussed the potential risks involved if you mix up your business and personal financial transactions as a member of a Limited Liability Company. To help avoid this, set up a business checking account with your bank. As long as this account is only used for business transactions, it should be much easier to make sure your finances are kept separate.

It can certainly be scary to do business in our litigious society today, but as we can see, if you take a few simple steps and manage your business in good faith, a small business setback does not have to automatically mean personal financial ruin as well.

Chapter 4:
Direct Ownership Real Estate Investment

We have briefly touched on the various ways to invest in real estate, and in the next chapters, we will discuss several of these options in depth. Real estate is one of the oldest forms of investment and is still as popular as ever. But most new real estate investors have no idea how many different ways there are to invest in real estate. Each investment type has its pros and cons, of course, and this book will give you a leg up on the competition since you will learn about many of them that your competition simply has not.

One of the best ways to build fortune is to find a niche and stick to it. Among the first lessons of business is not to try to be all things to all people; find what you excel at in business and stick to that.

But, before we dive in, another word of caution about protecting your money. *All* investment comes with risk; that's why it's not just called "free money." To state it one more time, you should almost never buy investment real estate properties in your own name; use a Limited Liability Company or any other structure that will protect your personal assets if the worst should happen!

With that out of the way again, let's dive right into this fascinating world.

Perhaps the most common type of real estate investment and the one most familiar to the new investor is called direct ownership real estate investment. This type of investment involves the highest potential reward but also the highest risk. It is also the most hands-on of the investment types, so if you are looking for a completely passive income, this may not be the strategy for you.

From apartment buildings to business complexes, you can find the kind of direct ownership investment property that fits you and your budget. The basic premise of direct ownership investment is that you purchase or build some piece of real estate and the difference between the cost of ownership of that property and the income from those occupying and using the property represents your profit or loss. That is the simplest description of this type of investment, but there may be more opportunities for direct ownership than you imagined.

Residential investments can include a house, an apartment building, a condo, a vacation home or any other property where someone will pay you to let them live on the property. Most of these are governed by an agreement between the tenant and the owner (or manager) called a "lease." A lease defines how long the tenant may occupy the property and how much they will pay for that, as well as any other responsibilities or rights that the tenant may have. Most leases in the US are for 12 months, which gives you the benefit of knowing how much you will receive from that property for 12 months, but if the market explodes in that area, you may not be able to take advantage of the increased earning potential during the lifetime of the lease.

Business real estate investments can include properties like strip malls, shopping malls or any other retail storefront. Not only can the owner of these types of property receive a monthly payment from the tenant in exchange for occupying the property, but many owners also receive a percentage of any sales generated by the tenant's business. This offsets the cost to the owner of keeping up the property and keeping it looking great.

Commercial real estate includes things like skyscrapers, office buildings, converted office spaces, etc. For an investor, these investments can be very appealing because often numerous companies will set up their offices within a single building, thus doing away with the risk to the owner of the building that he or she will receive no rent if one company goes belly up. In addition, commercial real estate usually involves multi-year leases, as opposed to only 12 months, which is customary in residential real estate. This comes with the same caveat as residential real estate in the case of the market heating up in that area, but the stable cash flow generated by multi-year leases makes up for that with many investors. In addition, in both commercial and residential real estate, a lease will also protect the investor against potential *declining* rental rates in the area.

Mixed-use real estate investments are gaining favor in many larger cities. These include any combination of the above-listed real estate investment types. In many cities, it is not uncommon to see a storefront on the ground floor of a building, offices on the middle floors, and private residences on the upper floors. As an investor, you will have an income stream from all of these sources. For larger investors, this can include setting up a large office complex with several commercial buildings surrounding it, such as restaurants, to serve the employees who work in the office complex. The appeal of mixed-use real estate investment is obvious due to the diversity of the income streams, but this type of investment usually requires significant resources, more than the typical investor will initially have.

Industrial real estate investments can include everything from a car lot or a car wash to a large warehouse leased by a company to distribute its product or any other special purpose property generating income from customers using that property. These types of investments often come with additional revenue streams, such as coin-operated vending machines, vacuum cleaners at a car wash, arcade video games—all of which maximize the investors' return.

These are the most obvious forms of direct ownership real estate investment, but there are several other ways to profit from investing in direct ownership of a real estate property. Many small investors, for example, will purchase a small apartment complex, such as a duplex or fourplex, and live in one unit while renting the other(s) out. This usually does not result in much, if any, direct profit, but the rental income will help build equity while you are living there for free. In the future, once the mortgage has been fully paid, most of the rental income will become a direct profit for you. Buying a piece of real estate or a building and then leasing it back to a tenant, such as a business, is more like a fixed income investment than an actual real estate investment. Basically, you are financing a building and allowing the income from the tenants to build equity for you.

Building equity in real estate is great, but it is not the only important thing to consider. You should never sacrifice liquidity in an attempt to build equity. This is a very easy way to end up in bankruptcy court. This can best be illustrated with two examples.

Let's imagine two homeowners—Holly and Mike. Now, Mike and Holly are like most Americans; they both want to own a home outright. This is the American dream, after all. But we will show you how it can be *disadvantageous* to make overpayments on your mortgage unless you are in a position to pay it off completely.

One of the most important lessons in business, or in life in general, is to keep enough cash on hand to withstand any setback, whether it be an illness or an economic downturn. Having this cash on hand is called being "liquid." As an investor, remaining liquid is vital.

Now, let's say you own the bank that holds the mortgages for Holly and Mike. Both own houses valued at $250,000. Well, Mike has never been a very good customer of your bank. He is up to his neck in credit card debt, has high car payments, is not always employed and is generally not liquid.

Holly, however, has been a dream customer. She has an outstanding credit score and often makes double payments or even triple payments on her mortgage. But Holly is not very liquid either.

Due to their differing payment habits, Mike still owes $200,000 on his house, and Holly only owes about $20,000 more. Both are eagerly awaiting the day when they will own their homes free and clear, but Holly is much closer to the goal.

But, catastrophe strikes both. For whatever reason, both are now out of work and are struggling to make ends meet each month. As the holder of their mortgages, your bank does not know that any of this has happened. All the bank knows is that it should receive a payment from

Mike and Holly by their respective due dates and for the correct amounts.

As the mortgage holder, your alarms should start to go off after about 2 missed payments. Of course, as a human being, you feel for their hardship, and you want to help, but at the end of the day, you are investing other people's hard-earned money, and you have an obligation to the investors to manage their money responsibly.

Eventually, the time comes when banking regulations require you to acknowledge that you are unlikely to be paid any further by either Mike or Holly. This is not good for the bank. The bank's profitability is damaged, the balance sheet has two large outstanding debts, and the investors are expecting you to act to protect their money. So, what do you do?

Your job, as the owner of the bank, is to get these loans back into the black as soon as possible. This is mostly accomplished by foreclosing on the property and auctioning it in an attempt to recoup your losses.

However, here is where things become counter-intuitive. For who is more likely to be foreclosed upon—Mike, who is a financial shambles and has very little equity in his home, or Holly, who made so many overpayments? Unfortunately, from a math perspective, this is an easy decision.

To recoup your losses on Mike's house, you would have to sell it for almost the full original loan amount of $250,000 to break even after the costs of the foreclosure, listing the house, auction fees, etc. At best, it will be a lengthy process to break even, and when it comes to your balance sheet, time is of the essence. Since Holly has made so many overpayments, she now only owes $20,000 on a house that was originally purchased for $250,000. If you foreclose on her, you can sell that property quickly at a very steep discount and recoup your $20,000 in bad debt.

Naturally, you feel for Holly and acknowledge that she did everything right, and perhaps it is not fair that she is the one to lose her house, and Mike is more likely to have his loan restructured on easier terms for him, but from an investment perspective it makes perfect sense. Investors are not only millionaires looking to increase their wealth, but they also consist of 401(k) and IRA retirement funds. Your duty to these investors is to guarantee them a stable return on their investments.

Letting Mike's house sit around on the market for months so that you can make little to no profit, and potentially lose money on the deal, is not good for your investors. Selling Holly's house on the market for 50% of its original selling price, on the other hand, should take only several weeks and ensures that your investors have recouped their money. Holly will lose a great deal more of her equity than if she had had time to list it herself on the market for a fair price, but the bank's balance sheet will remain clean.

The sad fact is the bank is going after Holly's house first. As Mike's lender, you know you are unlikely to achieve anything positive by going after his house, so you are more likely to work with him and restructure his payments somehow to keep his loan in good standing on the books. There are regulations specifying how far the bank can go to legitimately keep Mike's loan on the books as a "good" loan, but within this framework, it is up to the bank how far it is willing to go to avoid having to write off this bad debt.

For both Mike and Holly, this could have been avoided by staying liquid. Never forget, the bank is not concerned with how much money you still owe them; it just wants its monthly payments, on time and in full, so that the loan remains healthy on the books.

Rather than making so many double and triple payments, Holly would have done better to put that money into a safe low-yield investment. This way, when disaster struck, she would have been able to withdraw those funds and continue to make her monthly payments with that money until she was back on her feet. And if it turned out that she would not be able to get back on her feet, she would have been able to sell the house at a fair market price, repay the bank the remainder of the loan, and pocket any remaining equity before the worst happened.

The danger of being liquid, however, is the temptation to spend that money. It is hard to avoid being tempted by an account with a large amount of money in it that is not designated for any other purpose. The desire will always be there to just dip a little into that account for other purposes and replace it later. The problem with this is that for most folks the replacement will never happen but the debt remains.

Liquidity is a vital strategy, but, as we can see, it requires a great deal of discipline. If you decide to take my advice and set aside money for a rainy day each month, which I hope you do, consider that money gone once it has been placed into your reserve fund, wherever you choose to store that money. Don't be tempted to take out "just a little" to spend on anything other than a house payment in an emergency situation. This is all that money should be used for.

Another danger of that rainy day fund is the temptation to make riskier investments to maximize your returns. But remember, this is not your investment capital; this is your emergency reserve. It is not meant to generate a large return, it is meant to be *there and safe* in the event you need it.

As an investor, one of the worst things that could happen is that you lose your investment because, due to a temporary hardship, you were unable to make the monthly payments on the property that was supposed to build the foundation of your financial future. Please don't be that investor;

remain liquid above nearly all else and don't touch your rainy day fund, unless it is raining *hard*.

Fix and Flip

With the explosion in popularity of reality TV personalities purchasing rundown houses, fixing them up, and then quickly flipping them for a tidy profit, "house flipping" has become one of the most common forms of direct ownership real estate investment, so much so that we will devote a much longer section to this topic.

First lesson, don't believe the hype. No matter what you see on TV, learning to fix and flip houses is neither easy nor quick, although it can be quite profitable. House flipping actually requires a fair amount of knowledge—much more than can be gained from taking a two-day course and watching reality TV—and a lot of work.

However, it can be done successfully, and, as with anything, the best way to learn is to do it. You will make mistakes, and you will learn from those and get better next time. It's how we learn. As long as you have followed my recommendation to protect yourself, your downside risk should be minimized. Is it easy to flip houses? Nope. But there are certain common mistakes that I will share here to help you avoid the major pitfalls and still walk away with a nice return. And, of course, the more you do it the better you will be at it.

What Exactly Is House Flipping?

Before we get into the actual process of house flipping, let's just take a closer look at what it actually is. The term "flipping houses" is used by most people to refer to the process of buying distressed properties at foreclosure auctions or short sales at a steep discount. As mentioned above, the bank is just trying to recoup its investment as fast as possible, so sale prices are usually well below market value. The investor will then quickly resell ("flip") the property to a homeowner closer to market value without doing many, if any, renovations. This is what house flipping actually is, and it can be profitable, but that's not the kind of house flipping we will discuss. That kind of house flipping relies on quick turnover and quick profits to be effective.

Wholesaling of real estate is often, wrongly, also referred to as flipping houses. The wholesaling of real estate is a process whereby the wholesaler makes a contract with a home seller to purchase the home and then "flips" that contract to a real estate investor for a profit. In other words, the wholesaler simply inserts himself as a middleman between buyer and seller. As a real estate investor, you may find real estate wholesalers to be a valuable asset, but this is also not the sort of flipping we will discuss.

Learning real estate investment, including house flipping, is not easy. It takes a lot of capital and a lot of hard work. In the sort of house flipping we will discuss here, you will need capital for the initial purchase of the property and capital to renovate the property to add value and maximize your return. Done correctly, this can be quite a great investment, but in the wrong market or with bad luck, it can also be risky.

One final word of caution before we dive in here: many contractors think that they can make their fortunes with house flipping, but this may be because their math is flawed. Contractors often make the mistake of investing their capital in a house, doing the remodel themselves, selling the property, and then counting the difference between what they invested and what they sold the property for as their profit.

The problem with this is that the contractor is not taking his *risk* into consideration. Let's say a contractor takes on a job for a real estate investor, for example, that would take 8 weeks and net him $30,000 in profit. This contractor has kept his employees busy for 8 weeks and had made $30,000 for his investment of time and resources. Now, let's say that the same contractor bought a distressed property, had his crew work on it for 8 weeks, and then resold the property for a $30,000 profit. The contractor has actually achieved nothing, except to put his money at risk. See, the contractor put his own capital at risk to invest in the project and made only the same amount of money he would have made by working for the real estate investor, whose job it is to put capital at risk.

So, if you are a contractor reading this because you want to move into real estate investing, make sure you will make more money flipping the house than you would have by simply being hired to do the remodel.

Now, the first step to successfully flipping houses profitably is to know where you stand financially. It is crucial to know exactly how much money you will have available to invest in your property and to renovate it and whether you will need to borrow money or take on investment partners to raise enough capital.

Finding investors is, of course, not always easy, but knowing what your financial situation is in advance is the most logical place to get started. Initially, to minimize your personal risk, you will want to invest as little of your own money as possible. Of course, this will dilute the profits that you will get personally, but it is far better to get only a share of the profits than nothing at all. Additionally, taking on a partner or investor who has experience with flipping houses will provide you with another resource to avoid the most devastating pitfalls.

The next step is to build a team you trust. This is the team that will help you find the properties, fix them up, and then sell them for a (hopefully) nice profit.

It is simply impossible to complete a house flip all by yourself and still remain profitable. So, build a dream team to help you wade through it faster than you could by yourself; you will then also have a team to put your head together with when things go wrong.

At first, your team (at a minimum) should consist of a real estate broker, a contractor, architect, accountant, money lender and your insurance expert. The collective wisdom of this team should make you profitable much faster than you could hope to achieve on your own. This is not the time to be stubborn or greedy. Bringing in help will make your life easier, no matter what level of experience you possess, and will make the ultimate profits much greater.

The next step is an obvious one but is easier said than done. You must find a suitable property to flip. If you have taken the valuable step of doing your homework and finding the most promising neighborhood to invest in, this will make your task even more challenging as your choice will be limited to that geographic area, but the right neighborhood can make or break an investment, so don't skimp on the homework.

The goal is to buy a property for a low price, accurately assess the remodel costs, and then sell it for a worthwhile profit. This is why you will need your team. The faster you can work your way through all these steps the more properties you will flip and the more money you will ultimately make.

A real estate broker or a real estate wholesaler will be critical resources in helping you find properties that will sell cheaply enough for you to make a profit.

I cannot stress this part enough: do the math. Like contractors forgetting to take their risk factor into account, more house flippers have been undone by flawed math than nearly any other factor.

When choosing whether to invest your money into a property, you will want to take a hardheaded look at the numbers. Make a realistic assessment of what the house will cost to obtain initially, how much it will cost to repair the home (here I always recommend budgeting for the worst-case scenario; this is not the time for wishful thinking), and what the house is likely to sell for once it has been renovated. As you are doing your math, don't forget to take into account the monthly costs of owning the house, such as taxes, maintenance fees, etc., until you can sell it.

If you have crunched all of these numbers together with your team and everybody agrees that you will make enough money off your collective investment to make it worthwhile, you have likely found your winner, and you should consider making an offer on it.

Another common mistake that flippers make is not managing the renovation with a tight leash. You should not micromanage your contractor, you chose that person for a reason, and you should trust them to handle and supervise the repairs; but it is your job to keep an eye on the repairs to ensure they are being done efficiently and on-budget.

The initial purchase price of the house will play a large role in your ultimate profits, but if you keep an eye on the renovations and your budget, this will make sure you get the full potential out of the house when you finally sell it.

In addition to letting your contractor work unsupervised, the second major mistake investors make when renovating their properties is over-renovating. At the end of the day, you are not going to be living in this home; you should not decorate it to suit your tastes. Your goal is to make the house desirable and profitable, so unless doing something to the house will make it significantly more valuable on the market, don't bother.

You must also know your market when it comes to managing the renovation. Even if a particular improvement would increase the value of the house by thousands of dollars, it may not be worth doing if the other houses in the neighborhood are not selling for as much money as you would hope to receive if you undertook that improvement.

Finally, the last tip when it comes to flipping houses is to work fast. Your profit depends on how fast you work. The longer your renovation takes and the longer your house sits on the market waiting for a buyer the smaller your profits. Every month that goes by sees more and more money out of your pocket for taxes, insurance costs, mortgage payments, utilities, and on and on. It all adds up, so the faster you can turn that house over the more profit you will ultimately make.

This does not mean you should do shoddy work or cut corners. Your workmanship should reflect your personal values and should add value to the property; the work should just be done as fast as possible.

Every property is different, of course, but you should budget for about 6 months from purchase to sale, with a few extra months of expenses added on to be on the safe side. So, make sure you can afford to wait that long for a return on your investment.

Many investors make the mistake of believing that house flipping can only be profitable in times of rapid real estate appreciation, but this is simply not so. If you choose your properties wisely, work quickly and efficiently while still putting out a product you can be proud of, fixing and flipping will always be a profitable endeavor for you.

Chapter 5:
Real Estate Investment Groups and Limited Partnerships

A real estate investment group is simply that—a group of partners who invest in real estate. This is similar to direct ownership real estate investment but is structured in a way that is less hands-on for the investor.

The different types of investments that are available to a real estate investment group are much the same as those available to a single investor. The difference lies in the fact that a real estate investment group provides only the capital investment.

They will usually hire a property management company to manage the properties for the investors in exchange for a percentage of the monthly income from the properties. When choosing your property management, choose wisely because your investment is only going to be as good as the people managing it.

These groups will also often serve as money lenders to established flippers who wish to take on a larger project. Here, too, the group will leave the day-to-day operations to the experts in exchange for a share of the profits.

For many investors who desire a less hands-on approach to investing but don't want to simply hand their money over to a mutual fund or some other sort of investment firm and passively observe the results, this can be an ideal option.

The profit margin will be smaller, of course, since investors must pay the experts to carry out day-to-day operations for them, but the risk is also significantly less than being a sole investor because it is spread out among a group of investors who allow real estate professionals to manage their investments for them.

There are many real estate investment groups out there to choose from. As always, it is your hard-earned money that you are investing, so it is your responsibility to do your homework and make sure you are choosing a real estate investment group that fits your needs and whose investments match the level of risk that you are looking for.

Many investors choose to form their own Real estate investment group by finding a group of like-minded friends to pool their resources with. When forming your group, it will be important for you to make sure that everybody is on the same page.

Another key point to remember is to make sure to keep a reserve of funds to cover the costs associated with any long-term vacant units. You don't want to lose your investment for lack of a couple hundred dollars a month.

Real estate limited partnerships can be another great investment opportunity if you are not looking to be a landlord. Real estate limited partnerships essentially invest money in developing new real estate properties, and the profit represents the difference between the cost of building the property and the price it eventually sells for.

These partnerships require little to no hands-on involvement, other than perhaps occasional meetings, and do not require you to be a landlord and deal with everything that comes along with that, although the profit will, again, be smaller.

Chapter 6:
Real Estate Investment Trusts

Not every investor wants to be even that hands-on with their real estate investments; many are looking for more of a passive investment. One of the more popular investments in the real estate investing community is called a Real Estate Investment Trust or REIT.

Real Estate Investment Trusts can be a convenient option for the average investor to profit from the real estate market without having to deal with the headache of direct property acquisition.

Prior to the 1960s, only the wealthiest individuals and corporations were in a financial position to invest in larger real estate projects, such as shopping malls, business complexes, hotels, skyscrapers, etc. Finally, with the Real Estate Investment Trust Act of 1960, Congress made these special companies exempt from corporate income taxes if they met certain conditions.

The reason Congress passed this was in an attempt to create an incentive for investors to pool their resources in the form of companies investing in large real estate projects. It was successful as the first Real Estate Investment Trust was created only three years later.

In exchange for these generous tax breaks, Real Estate Investment Trusts must pass a fourfold test each year to maintain their status.

First, the trust must distribute at least 90% of its annual taxable income, except for capital gains, each year to its shareholders as dividends.

Second, the trust must have at least 75% of its assets invested in real estate, though this can also include investing in other Real Estate Investment Trusts, mortgage loans, and government securities.

Third, the trust must obtain 75% of its income from real estate, including rents, interest from mortgage loans or profits from selling real estate.

Finally, the Real Estate Investment Trust must have at least 100 shareholders, and no small group of shareholders can own more than half of the shares. The regulations forbid a group of five shareholders or less from owning more than 50% of all shares. This prevents too much influence from collecting in the hands of a powerful few.

One of the benefits of investing in a Real Estate Investment Trust is that REITs are required by regulations to distribute almost all of their income (at least 90%) as dividends. This does come with some tax implications for you as an investor, however; for example, your dividends will be taxed at a higher rate than common stocks, but this can be a great addition to your investment portfolio if you can buy in at the right price and have enough margin of safety.

Another advantage is that you can avoid double-taxation, allowing more investor capital to compound.

You will have a professional, dedicated management team running the day-to-day operations of the business in a way that would perhaps exceed your personal level of expertise.

Unlike directly-owned real estate, Real Estate Investment Trusts are fairly liquid, meaning you can cash out quickly if necessary, while a house or condo may sit on the market for months before selling.

Due to their relatively high level of cash dividends compared to the market, Real Estate Investment Trusts provide more portfolio stability than many other investments because they are less likely to sink as low as common stock in the case of a market downturn.

Investing in Real Estate Investment Trusts, investors with only a few thousand dollars to invest can diversify their investment across different geographic areas or across different areas of specialization. Investing only in direct ownership, you would need a much larger pool of capital to accomplish this.

To get started investing in a Real Estate Investment Trust, simply decide what sort of real estate you would like to invest your money in, do your homework to find a REIT that matches your interests and will protect your money, and contact your broker about making the investment. If you do decide that investing in Real Estate Investment Trusts is right for you, just remember that REITs are not just a collection of real estate properties; they are actually businesses that you are investing in, so make sure you analyze them as such when doing your research.

Conclusion

Thank you for making it through to the end of this book, let's hope it was informative and able to provide you with all of the tools you need to achieve your goals whatever they may be.

The world of real estate investing is a fascinating one. Many fortunes have been made with a relatively small initial investment.

Real estate investment is perfect for those who are not looking to simply throw money at a professional broker to invest and hope for the best. It offers a great opportunity to invest your money with a good chance of making a decent return with you in charge of how your money is invested. Unless you choose to make your investment in a Real Estate Investment Trust or something similar, you will at least have some control over how your money is invested, and if you choose direct ownership, you will have complete control. The best part is there are investments for any level of involvement you're looking for, so if it's a totally passive income that you want, then a REIT may be perfect for you. After all, it's your money, and you should invest it in the way that makes you most comfortable.

With thousands of years of tradition backing it, property ownership can give you security, social standing, and, not least of all, a roof over your head. And who doesn't want that? As an investor in real estate, not only can you hope to make a worthwhile profit from your investment, you can also help your buyers achieve *their* goal of property ownership.

There are few other investments that are quite so tangible or immediate as real estate. When you own a piece of property, you can visit it, touch it, show it to your friends; it is *there*. Many investors love this about real estate. The property is there as proof of your investment, and you get all the pride of ownership, even if you are not going to live in the property.

The next step is to get started! As with any game, you can only win if you are on the field, playing. And the more you play the better you will become.

Finally, if you found this book useful in any way, a review on Amazon is always appreciated!

www.ingramcontent.com/pod-product-compliance
Lightning Source LLC
Chambersburg PA
CBHW030443220526
45464CB00006B/2391